TATTINGSTONE PRESS

MAVIS WENT TOO
Females Under Fire, 1600–1918

ANNETTE BAILEY

Published by Tattingstone Press

ISBN: 1539608328

ISBN-13: 978-1539608325

CONTENTS

ACKNOWLEDGEMENTS

Thanks must go to my husband, novelist Garry Kilworth, who has given huge encouragement to all that I have ever undertaken, especially this book where he also gave technical and editorial advice. To Keith Brooke who helped when I needed it. Thanks also to Lesley Levene, Colin Waters and Major John Spires for their helpful comments, to TACA and Julia Chaplin who gave me useful information. Also all the people who enabled me to use illustrations, especially Gavin Glass of the Royal Irish Rifles Museum, Melissa Atkinson of Friends House and Geoff Spender at the Imperial War Museum.

ILLUSTRATIONS AND PHOTOGRAPHS

ILLUSTRATIONS
Julia Temple, Tattingstone, Suffolk.

PHOTOGRAPHS

Page 31: James (Miranda) Barry. Wellcome Library, London.

Page 33: Florence Nightingale. National Portrait Gallery

Page 34: Mary Seacole. National Portrait Gallery

Page 35: 'To Pack Up Her Tatters And Follow The Drum': Thomas Rowlandson 1805, Yale Centre for British Art: Paul Mellon Collection.

Page 42: Regimental School, Poona 1852. Royal Irish Rifles.

Page 47: Light Dragoon Barracks Room, 1788. National Army Museum.

Page 57: Children's Tug of War on a homeward bound troop ship—boys versus girls. *The Graphic*, 19th October 1887. TACA.

Page 57: 'Her Majesty Addressing the Wives and Children of The Household Cavalry and Reservists at Windsor'. November 29th 1899. They are about to leave for the 2nd Boer War1900. *The Graphic*, 1887. TACA.

Page 58: 'Married Without Leave, Left behind on the Departure of the Regiment'. *The Graphic*, 12th January 1884. TACA.

Page 66: Gertrude Bell. Newcastle University Archives.

Page 70: Flora Sandes. Public domain.

Page 73: Inhabitants Evacuated from Marne—Friends House.

Page 75: FAU—Hospital Staff, Dunkirk 1914—Friends House.

Page 87: 'Women of Britain Say Go'. UK Government, public domain.

Page 89: Gun Factory at the Royal Arsenal, Woolwich London, 1918. Imperial War Museum.

INTRODUCTION

THERE HAS ALWAYS BEEN FEMALE involvement in military campaigns. I became aware of this when I was doing some research into military families in Britain. My brief was to look into the ways present day children of military families adapted to their lifestyle. I had very limited space to devote to military families in history, much as I found the subject fascinating.

My surprise was profound when I read the accounts of women who had been highly active in the military on behalf of Britain throughout many of the wars and political changes that took place in the past. In spite of having been in a military family myself (a camp follower if you like) and of having worked overseas with military families I had assumed, without really thinking too hard, that the women who lived as soldiers and sailors and took on many other roles were chancing their luck at the barrack gates.

The intention of this book is to highlight the achievements and motivations of the many women who served and were part of the British military machinery between the 1600s to the end of World War I. It is an overview, by no means comprehensive, which considers the different roles taken by many thousands of women.

I have tried to answer the following questions. Who were these women? What roles did they take? Why did they go to war? Why were they so necessary to the early British military machine?

I found that the cross-dressing women of the early ballads had always been present in the military scenario. Alongside these were the less romantic but very useful camp followers, who cropped up all over the world. Where would the men have been without the hard pressed and often enterprising sutlers supplying all the goods needed by any army? I would not want to forget, the unfortunate wives of the late 1800s, also the spies, nurses and hard working women of World War I.

The British Army and Navy became entities around the mid 1600s so it is a good place to start. Women would have been involved before that date, but we don't know as much about them. Some women served openly, some clandestinely, many were wives or girlfriends. They were always there and seldom acknowledged.

Where there is evidence of named women I have written about them as individuals. Otherwise I have gathered them together under the collective name of 'Mavis' for reasons of simplicity and in order to emphasise that they were often what would seem to be ordinary females.

MY INTRODUCTION TOUCHES UPON THREE ancient female warriors. They make a fine primer because they show that a woman could captain a ship or lead an army doing a good, if not a better job than the men. Their stories like many others in this book are amazing and I feel they deserve an airing in the opening pages.

One woman who was not British is a fine early example of women's accomplishments in a man's world. Since we are talking about female military heroines the story of **Artemisia** is well documented and will set us nicely on the path towards her British counterparts. The Greek historian, Herodotus, in his work *The Histories* recounts the story of her exploits in the Greek–Persian Wars of 480 BC.

She was one of the most esteemed commanders in the navy of the Persian King Xerxes, in his wars against the Greeks.

According to Herodotus, Artemisia twice gave good counsel to the Persian King Xerxes advising him not to enter into a battle. On both occasions he ignored her and consequently suffered defeat. As a result he had great respect for her counsel and made her captain of one of his warships. His other naval commanders were required to heed her advice in future conflicts. The attack vessels of the time had sails but these were not usually employed during battle. Instead the 'triremes' were propelled by lines of rowers, three tiers of them. Their aim was to smash into the sides of enemy vessels, the prows of these great craft being reinforced with heavy bronze rammers.

Although she successfully captained one of these ships and crew Artemisia had a strong survival instinct and did not trust the courage or the expertise of some of the male captains of the other Persian ships. At one point in a battle against the Greek triremes, her vessel was in danger of being trapped. To extricate her ship she deliberately rammed another craft on her own Persian side to fool the enemy into thinking she was a Greek ship. This tactic was successful but one can only imagine her unpopularity with her Persian allies.

WHILE WE ARE DEALING WITH ancient times there are two British heroines who are well acknowledged in historical records. They were both skilled at negotiation and leadership, in that they were successful in unifying normally hostile tribes against a common enemy. Both of them were the widows of great warriors and they took to leadership in war to continue the role that their dead husbands had taken before them.

The warrior Queen, **Boudicca**, ruled in East Anglia after her husband's death. The Roman writer Tacitus tells us how her husband's will and testament was ignored by the Romans. He had left his wife Boudicca his properties, which the Romans confiscated.

When Boudicca, who was a young woman in her thirties, protested at the misappropriation of her rights, she was whipped and her teenage daughters were raped. Being furious she retaliated with great martial success, rocking the Roman expeditionary army on its heels and almost destroying it completely.

Her image is wonderful. She must have cut such a magnificent figure in her chariot at the head of her Celtic hordes. Her red hair and brilliant gold torque would have splendidly displayed her beauty, status and wealth. Using her charisma and showing strong leadership Queen Boudicca managed to unite the tribes of the Trinovantes, Iceni and others in Norfolk, Suffolk and Cambridgeshire. Together under her command they successfully waged a war against Roman occupation defeating the Roman army at Colchester and then at London in AD 60 and 61. Eventually she was overcome in a battle at St Albans.

SO, TO MY LAST WOMAN warrior, who though similar in approach, is less well known than Queen Boudicca but is actually more historically important. **The Lady of the Mercians, Queen Aethelflaed**, oldest child of Alfred the Great is mentioned in the *Anglo-Saxon Chronicles*. She was attacked by a group of Danes on her way to her wedding and subsequently held a serious grudge against the Viking invaders. After becoming widowed in 911 her father, King Alfred, saw her potential and insisted she take over her dead husband's role as leader of the army. To this end she established garrisons in Hereford and Gloucester and re-built the walls at Chester.

Aethelflaed saw her main task as uniting the Saxon armies of Mercia and Wessex, even though these two kingdoms had been at war with each other for many years. She had already proved herself a competent military leader but she enhanced her reputation when she led her troops to Leicester where they managed to defeat an invading force greater than her own with hardly a battle. The Vikings surrendered without a fight in spite of their stronghold being well defended. Clearly, news of her victories had gone before her to ensure her victory.

She achieved an enduring peace between the tribes and together with her victories over the Vikings succeeded in bringing together most of the England we know today. She ruled with her brother Edward for eight years. Their heads are to be found together on coins from that period.

At her death Saxons and surprisingly, also the Vikings mourned her passing. Thus we note that those fearsome Norsemen who had attacked along English shores for so long, appreciated a high-born woman with skill enough to give her country's enemies a good battle and then after the event, make peace.

SO MUCH FOR THE EXAMPLES given by our ancient heroines!

This book in part is about some women who did great things in history. Mavis, our ordinary woman was certainly present at conflicts where the women protected their homes and townships in the absence of the men-folk. There are two ancient orders of knighthood, again not British, granted to women for acts of valour while their men were away fighting another battle.

Spain and France have produced some formidable bands of women throughout their history. It seems that when necessary, the women fought well and were impressively successful.

In 1149 AD the **Order of the Hatchet** (Order de Hacha) was presented to the women and children of Tortosa, Catalonia, Spain, by Don Raymond, Earl of Barcelona. This occurred when the women and their children were left alone and undefended by the men of the town. They fell under siege to the attacking Moors and although they sent for assistance to the Earl, he was unable to spare any troops and he told them to surrender.

This, the women of Tortosa refused to do, believing that they would be killed or raped and their children taken into slavery. So rather than give in to that situation, they donned male armour and took the weapons their men folk had left behind.

They successfully defended the walls of the town against the Moors with courage and fortitude. Eventually the siege was raised and the Earl found himself obliged to grant them various honours. One of these privileges meant the women were no longer required to pay taxes and they must have been delighted to be also permitted to keep for themselves their own jewellery and the effects of their dead husbands.

The story is somewhat the same for **Jeanne Fourquet,** who also became known as '**Jeanne Hachette**' after her favourite weapon, the hatchet. In 1472 she and some loyal French women assisted Commander Louis de Balagny in preventing an assault on Beauvais by the Duke of Burgundy.

After the battle a grateful King Louis XI rewarded the women by instituting a parade named '***Procession of the Assault***' in gratitude for their services. The women were allowed to march at the head of a column in front of the men:

> 'The Burgundian women carried themselves in the manner of Military Knights'
> (Cardinal; Orders of Knighthood and the Holy See 1983)

Hopefully they also were allowed to keep their own jewellery and the effects of their husbands. We learn that once more they were rewarded by being relieved of paying taxes. The parade became an annual event.

Similarly the women of the high fortress town of Casaris, Southern Spain, managed to repel an attack by French forces during the Peninsular War. Their men were away fighting elsewhere. It was the only area apart from Cadiz that Napoleon had not been able to take. This time there was no reward of knighthoods, though the king was said to be extremely grateful.

In England Henry Addington, first Viscount of Sidmouth, received a petition from the women of Neath in 1803, responding to the threat of a French invasion. The females requested permission:

> '...to defend ourselves as well as the weaker women and children amongst us. There are in this town about 200 women who have been used to hard labour all the days of their lives, such as working in coal pits, on the high roads, tilling the ground etc. If you would grant us arms, that is light pikes...we do assure you we could in short learn our exercise.'

Even though the women pleaded with Addington their request was denied.

'…we are not trifling with you but serious in our proposal,'

One would hope that Henry Addington might not need the assistance of those women, ever again.

(Myrna Trustram; Women of the Regiment 2008)

SO MUCH FOR GROUP SITUATIONS where women took up arms to defend their homes and families. It is interesting to consider whether the roles women took were by choice or circumstance.

Mavis could have been a woman living or working in a port area or in an area where there was military activity. She may have had humble origins and joined the military to seek a loved one or escape oppression or ill treatment at home. She could have achieved fame as one of the women who went to sea dressed as a man to be later immortalised in the ballads that became so popular. Alternatively she may have been a high born lady who wanted adventure and freedom from the constraints of her class and times.

Whatever role she took, Mavis was present at every military outpost in all early British military campaigns worldwide. The vast majority, tens of thousands, were ordinary women who worked, lived, gave birth and died undertaking many important roles within the military.

Mavis and her children will often have been described as 'camp followers' a term frequently misunderstood. One of the intentions of this book is to clarify their roles and give due recognition to the services they did give to the British forces.

WORLD WAR I WAS WELL under way before women were officially paid by the War Office to do some of the work normally undertaken by the men in uniform. Because the coming of women's military services marks a recognition of what women had always done and because that acknowledgement led in part to women gaining the right to vote, this book concludes in 1918.

There is excellent documentation of women's roles throughout World Wars I and II and up to this present day. There is no need to attempt to add to the information already available.

CHAPTER 1

A UNIFORMED APPROACH

NAMED WOMEN 1700–1900

THE INTENTION OF THIS BOOK is to demonstrate that war has never been solely a man's domain, fought by male soldiers and sailors. Mavis, our ordinary woman has always made a contribution. She was not awarded medals and was not always fed and paid. She clearly did not seek glory and was seldom given recognition for her efforts.

So what were her motivations? A handful of the women who lived and worked as soldiers and sailors did gain respect, high rank and positions of responsibility. Most of the early heroines of music hall fame had to be satisfied with living a life that suited them.

The downside of such a chosen lifestyle was that they had to live with a false identity. This had its drawbacks and if they were discovered by those in command, they were made to leave the service.

In this chapter the women who are named are representatives of many more. They tended to use one or several aliases in order to protect their identity. That they did exist is beyond dispute since there are adequate diaries and letters to support their activities. Their exploits are documented in folk law and ballad in such numbers that one cannot doubt the authenticity of their situation though on occasions the detail may change. They are immortalized in over 1,000 bawdy theatre songs which were usually performed in rather patronising tones.

A number of these earlier examples tell of women going to war to find a loved one. I have here a selection of stories that I find most interesting in order to show some of the situations into which the women took themselves. Their stories are well told and their gender was usually thought to be male by those around them.

It is difficult to imagine how these women did disguise their female gender. In fact there are stories of women making contraptions from leather belts and piping which enabled them to 'pee' standing up. Even so, one would hope they did not perform their toilet close enough for inspection by the man standing next to them. One can imagine them replying to an obvious astonished enquiry, *'Wounded you know, in that last battle, the surgeon fitted me up with this'*.

A common, thread that links many of these tales is that the women longed to escape domesticity or the tyranny of a husband, father or guardian. Gaining a financially rewarding occupation and male privileges are likely to have also had an appeal to some of these independent and resourceful women. The following are listed more or less chronologically although some of the stories do seem timeless.

There are some excellent accounts of the following women and others to be found in **Julie Wheelwright's** 1990s book *Amazons and Military Maids*.

Christian Davies is typical and she took the traditional path that appears in the music hall ballads. Born in 1667, in Dublin, of a brewer family then known by her birth name as **Christian Cavanagh**, as well as **Christian Davies**, she inherited a public house and married her employee Richard Welch. The couple had three sons.

One day, Richard suddenly disappeared and in order to search for him Christian changed her name to **Christopher Welch**, donned male clothes and in 1697 enlisted in Captain Tichbourne's Company of Foot to set out to find him. She was known to her comrades simply as 'Kit' for the next nine or more years.

In 1706 she was successfully reunited with Richard for a short while. He claimed he had been pressed into the army and had not been able to contact her but since he was a known scoundrel and womaniser she no longer wanted to be married to him. She did re-marry him later.

She clearly enjoyed her military life and left the infantry to serve on horseback as a dragoon with various regiments, including the Scots Greys. Fortunately she and her husband remained close friends and he kept her secret so she could continue in her male role. That she managed to conceal her gender for many more years is quite surprising although she clearly went to considerable lengths to do so. She was eating, sleeping and urinating as a man. A prostitute even claimed she had fathered a child, a situation Christian seems to have found quite amusing.

After fighting in the Battle of Ramilles she suffered a severe head injury which required surgery and under the knife of the military surgeon, her secret was unveiled. She was forced to leave the army.

She must have gained considerable respect amongst her colleagues since on leaving the military she was given new clothes as a parting gift by the officers of the Scots Guards. She thereafter worked as a sutler selling meat and wine to the troops until 1712.

In later life she married once more and finding herself in sad circumstances as a widow, pregnant and having no means of income, she visited Lord Marlborough, her old commander. He gave her a letter to present to Queen Anne verifying her twelve year service to the crown and to her being the widow of two soldiers. She clearly impressed Queen Anne since she was granted a military pension. After further marriages she died in 1739 and was given the honour of being buried at the Pensioners' College in Chelsea where there was a three gun volley fired over her grave at the time of her funeral.

SOMETIMES THE MEN WERE COMPLETELY unaware of the gender of their female companions but in a number of cases it must have been acknowledged by close companions that the wearer of the uniform was female. Undoubtedly the fact was not seen as too important by the men with whom she worked especially if she was amenable and worked well. It was only when it became obvious to those of higher rank that the gender issue became insurmountable, requiring the woman to leave the service.

Some of the women quoted above, had close female relationships with other women while in their military roles. This could have been due to their sexual orientation or because they needed to have comfort and safety. Whatever the reason, they often returned to more traditional roles as wives and mothers once they left the service.

The motivation for **Hannah Snell** was somewhat similar to that of 'Kit' Cavanagh (Christian Davies). Hannah was born in Worcester in 1723 to a naval family. Three of her brothers were sailors, and five of her sisters had married military men. She married a Dutch sailor, James Summs, in 1744, who went to sea leaving her when she was six months pregnant. The child died and she chose to go in search of him wearing her brother-in-law's clothes.

Using the name James Gray, she enlisted in the Royal Navy and was ordered aboard the sloop of war, the *Swallow,* in 1745. She was wounded in the Battle of Pondicherry but recovered only to find that her estranged husband had died. She subsequently spent several more years as a sailor.

Only later did she resume her female identity to become a stage performer. She wrote and sold her memoirs, remarried and had a son. She died in1792.

Mary Anne Talbot, born in 1778 in Lincoln's Inn Fields, London, was the illegitimate daughter of Lord William Talbot. When her mother died she was put in the charge of a guardian, the disreputable Captain Bowen, who changed her name to **John Taylor** and enlisted her on his ship sailing to Santa Domingo. She was given the role of drummer boy and was taken to Flanders in 1792 where she participated in the capture of Valenciennes in 1793.

She deserted, making the break from her odious guardian, and successfully managed to become assigned to a British ship, the *Brunswick,* serving under Captain John Harvey. On receiving a wound she was taken prisoner by the French, only being freed in 1796. It was then that her luck ran out since she was taken by a press gang which resulted in her true identity being disclosed. Mary Anne Talbot, alias John Taylor, was then obliged to abandon her military life so she capitalised on her experience and worked for a while in the theatre.

She later learnt she should have received an inheritance from one of her original guardians, a Mr Sucker. Realising the money would have been spent she vowed to get revenge and in her male clothing tracked down the deceitful Mr Sucker, drew her sword and revealed her female identity. Mr Sucker died of shock, it seems, shortly after the confrontation. Mary Anne died at the relatively young age of 30.

THERE IS NO RECORD OF why **Isabel Gunn**, born 1781 to crofters in the Orkneys, chose to sign up with the Canadian Hudson Bay Fur Trading Company, an outpost run on military lines, in 1806. There are ballads and stories a plenty in Canada but the truth of her situation seems hard to gain. It is said she dressed as a man, took the name **John Fubister** and with the ship's company sailed to what was to become Canada. She later travelled, with other sailors by canoe 1,800 miles along the

Albany and Red Rivers to Pembina Post. During the journey across Canada she had secretly become pregnant by a John Scaith who did not want to be involved with the child.

It seems her disguise was revealed when she gave birth. Her life as John Fubister came to a sudden end and her son was heralded as the first white child born in Canada. She worked for a year at the trading post at Fort Albany eventually, reluctantly returning with her son to Orkney 1809.

A WOMAN KNOWN AS **William Brown** is believed to have been the first female from Jamaica to serve in the Royal Navy. 'William' gained so much respect from officers aboard the *Queen Charlotte* (110 guns), she was made 'Captain of the Fore-top' due to her agility when climbing the rigging. An Annual Report for 1815 tells us that she served as a seaman in the Royal Navy for up to 11 years and gained considerable prize money. She had joined following a quarrel with her husband and left the service when the ship came to her home port and he denounced her as a woman.

CLEARLY QUEEN VICTORIA WAS AWARE of female involvement aboard ships. The British government in 1847 suggested she award a Naval General Service Medal to all living survivors of major sea battles fought between 1793 and 1840. Her wording when asking for applicants read '...*without any reservation as to sex*'.

The award was to be distributed by Sir Byam Martin who was appointed by the Admiralty to do the job. He was made aware of an application for **Jane Townsend** who was aboard the *Defiance*, at the Battle of Trafalgar 1805, and also **Ann Hopping** and **Mary Anne Riley**, both of whom participated in the 'Battle of the Nile'. All had evidenced exemplary performances during the action. Sadly all female applications were refused. None of them received their medals. Sir Byam claimed that if these women were awarded the medals there would be numerous applications of the same nature. Women aboard ship were clearly viewed with suspicion by those in high places.

ONE OF THE MOST AMAZING stories of a woman living a successful military life is that of **James (Miranda) Stuart Barry**, born **Mary Ann Bulkley** sometime between 1789–1799. Barry will be referred to as a man henceforth since that is the way he lived almost all his life, taking the name **James Barry** from his uncle who was an artist. There is some evidence that the family were in compliance with this arrangement in order for Barry to qualify as a medical doctor, a profession completely closed to women at the time.

Graduating from Edinburgh University Medical School, Guys and St Thomas's hospitals James Barry qualified as a surgeon and served in the British Army in India, Africa, Canada and the Crimea. While in Africa, Barry successfully performed the first Caesarean section operation by a British surgeon where both mother and child survived.

Wherever he went he worked to improve the conditions of soldiers and local native people by campaigning for the supply of clean water and good nutrition. Having a good bedside manner towards his patients he tended to work in his own way. However, he was known to be somewhat insubordinate towards those in command for whom he frequently had little respect.

Florence Nightingale reported that he had been very rude and disrespectful towards her when they met while she was at Scutari Hospital, Constantinople, Turkey where she was busy organising the training and transport of nurses to the Crimea.

Clearly the pair had much in common as both of them were trying to improve the situation for the soldiers, so a better understanding between the two of them could have been advantageous to both. Barry just lacked the ability to give Florence the sort of respect she expected.

That was not the only situation that caused him grief. Several of his postings to alternative areas were as a result of a fall-out with his superiors. It is noted that he, unsurprisingly, was required to fight several duels as a result of people questioning his voice, demeanour or professionalism.

He was normally accompanied by his manservant John and his dog and they led an abstemious life. He did not drink alcohol or eat meat.

James (Miranda) Barry

By the end of his career he had risen to the lofty position of Inspector General in charge of all military hospitals. In 1864 Barry retired to England and died of dysentery in 1865. The charlady of the boarding house where he was staying, Sophia Bishop, performed the last offices and she let it be known after the funeral that Doctor Barry was indeed female. There exists a communication between George Graham, the registrar who had become aware of the charlady's claim, and

Major D.R. McKinnon, the doctor who had issued the death certificate on which Barry was identified as male.

McKinnon replying to George Graham wrote the following letter :

Sir

I have been intimately acquainted with the doctor (Barry) for a good many years, both in London and the West Indies and I never had any suspicion that Dr Barry was a woman. I attended him during his last illness. On my visit following Dr Barry's death there was a woman who performed at the last offices for Dr Barry waiting to speak to me. Amongst other things she said that Dr Barry was a female and that I was a pretty doctor not to know this and she would not like to be attended by me. I informed her that it was none of my business whether Dr Barry was male or female, and that I thought that he might be neither, viz. an imperfectly developed man. She then said that she had examined the body, and (it) was a perfect female and further that there were marks of him having had a child when very young. I then enquired—how have you formed that conclusion. The woman pointing to the lower part of her stomach said 'From the stretch marks here. I am a married woman and the mother of nine children so I ought to know'.

D.R. McKinnon goes on to say that he thought the woman was trying to obtain money. He clearly preferred his explanation to the possibility that Dr Barry had been female and he had been duped.

FLORENCE NIGHTINGALE BECAME WELL KNOWN in the 1850s by people from all walks of life. She made a huge difference to the well-being of incapacitated soldiers in the Crimean War. Although not a trained nurse and given that she never actually put foot on the war-torn Crimean peninsula, she highlighted the need to have efficient administration to deal with casualties and the men's welfare generally. It was she who provided for the transport and nursing of wounded and sick troops at the Crimea. She arranged for them to be conveyed in ships from the Crimea to Scutari Hospital in Constantinople, her base. Her contributions are well-documented and she paved the way for the formation of some very excellent nursing services.

Florence Nightingale

ONE WOMAN AT LEAST DID go purposefully to the Crimean war zone to tend the sick and wounded. Her part in that conflict has in the past been overlooked in favour of Florence Nightingale. **Mary Seacole**, a nurse of Scottish and Jamaican parentage, learned her nursing skills in the nursing home run by her mother.

In 1854 having heard of the dreadful plight of soldiers in the Crimea she approached the War Office and asked for permission and funds to set up a hospital on the peninsula. She was refused.

Undaunted she financed her own journey and set up **The British Hotel**, near Balaclava, where she nursed and fed sick or convalescent officers (the rank and file having been sent to Constantinople on Florence Nightingale's hospital ships). She also visited the battleground, sometimes under fire, to tend the wounded. The name the troops used for her was **Mother Seacole**.

She was indeed remarkable but not the only woman who nursed casualties during the Crimean War. There were the accompanying wives of soldiers who had always performed those tasks. Mary was unique in being a woman alone who used her meagre savings to travel and set up her '*hospital*' having no reason for putting her life at risk except caring for hurt men who were a long way from home. Mary returned to England in 1857, destitute.

Mary Seacole

To help her financially, a newspaper article appeared in the *Times* and caused an outcry which resulted in a 'benefit festival'. This attracted thousands of people who raised money for her old age. She spent it writing her memoirs.

CHAPTER 2

AND THE REST

WOMEN AND CHILDREN AT THE GATES

THE ROMANCE, DANGER AND EXCITEMENT experienced by the love-lorn maidens of the last chapter or the success of the dedicated Doctor Barry did not always give a true picture of military life for women. These accounts deny the importance of the more humdrum work Mavis undertook in her wider role as representative of many thousands of women.

The Oxford Companion to Military History (2001) by Richard Holmes uses the term 'camp follower', to refer to women and children of soldiers who followed the army from place to place to augment the services needed by the army.

Many of these women received some payment for their domestic, nursing and provisioning services. Some fought alongside the men. They were paid locally by the Commander of their regiment. Some were wives with children and a few would have been prostitutes but not as many as were supposed by some historians. Women were an essential part of every force's logistic capability.

War was seldom glorious for Mavis and the families of the forces. It did produce heroines and many women of great character. Where there is evidence of their involvement this chapter aims to look at the roles taken by women who were connected to the British army or navy, whether by intent or circumstance. It is necessary to now look at the situations under which they operated.

There were undoubtedly many women who lived within or on the periphery of a military encampment. Their numbers would have been far greater than those of the men. Mavis our ordinary woman, would have worn any clothing or military uniforms she found and would also have used weapons if they were available to her. She needed to be able to scavenge and was on some occasions accused of looting in the same manner as the men. Mavis was active at home, at sea and when accompanying an army on colonial service abroad.

Because of the loose nature of warfare some women simply became involved in the fighting and fought alongside the men. Some chose to fight and wanted to be part of the action. Some were wives officially on the strength of the regiment and required to work for their keep. Some were licensed sutlers providing food and liquor to the men. The sutlers worked independently and were paid for what they provided to the regiment. Many more were unlicensed and provided liquor of an illicit nature.

Women were an essential part of the capability of every military operation in early times. They undertook the many jobs needed to keep an army operational by cooking, laundering, sewing and nursing the sick.

In the retreat of British troops from Kabul, Afghanistan (known as the Massacre of Elphinstone's Army) in 1842 the official reports tell us that approximately 16,000 personnel were slain. It is too often assumed by casual historians that these were all fighting men. This is a false postulation. In fact there were only 4,000 soldiers bearing arms; the greatest number of those were Indian Sepoys, fighting alongside some 700 British troops. There were a number of auxiliary workers: saddlers, harness makers, armourers, carpenters and blacksmiths. The vast majority of those slaughtered, some 12,000, were women and children doing the necessary work which kept the army operating.

Rudyard Kipling, the writer of fiction, fondly known as the People's Laureate, was born and worked in India as a newspaper reporter. He drew on his experiences in Lahore, during the 1880s and 1890s, to frequently mention women and children in his stories. Although he does a fine job describing the rather spoilt and bored officers' ladies, he also writes of 'camp followers' on

many occasions. He clearly liked the common soldiers and their families:

> 'So (the regiment) went northward, ever northward, past droves and droves of camels, armies of camp followers and legions of laden mules'
>
> (*The Drums of the Fore and Aft*)

There was limited understanding in high places within the British establishment of the roles of the accompanying women. How far they were appreciated rather depended on who was reviewing the situation.

Myrna Trustram in her book *Women of the Regiment* (2008), gives us information about the situation of women on the war front and also of those left behind when the regiment moved on.

Here is a comment made by General James Murray on the women at the siege of Quebec in 1760 :

> 'The King victuals the women in order to render them useful to the men.'

There is an illustration by Paul E Kopperman of the role played by the women and families. He writes of those who accompanied the troops in the second half of the 18th century:

> 'Their most common function was laundering. In Garrison they often cooked for company or hired themselves out as servants to officers and their families... As a matter of routine or under orders they sewed and mended uniforms... In addition to their regular duties, some of them were called upon to herd the cattle and sheep that accompanied armies on the march... Army wives (not those of the officers of course), faced the prospect of being ordered to serve in hospitals...usually as nurses, sometimes as cooks, cleaning women or laundresses.'

Not only were women present at campaigns on land, they were aboard ship too. A piece by Admiral George Vernon Jackson tells of his experience at sea when he was a midshipman serving aboard the *Lapwing* in 1801. He recalled:

> 'Whilst getting the ship off the Shoal, it was amusing to see how some women—forty or fifty who were on board exerted themselves at the ropes.'

Another sea emergency focused a spotlight on work undertaken by invisible females. The *Horatioran* had run onto a needle rock off Guernsey and began to leak badly. The captain headed for port, racing against the water rushing into the hold. Later he praised the ship's women, who:

'Rendered essential service in thrumming the sail'

This technique required the women to rough up the surface of the sail and work-in short pieces of rope yarn to make it more absorbent. The sail was then lowered over the hole in the ship's bottom to slow the leak.

During the Peninsular War many soldiers lived side by side with local women who followed the regiment. A wife (possibly not officially married) may not have been British or even speak English.

'If well behaved some of these women were allowed to embark for England with a view to eventually being married.'

All the accompanying women shared in the hardship of seafaring and campaigning on land. They would have been subject to the harsh punishments that were inflicted upon the men. Many would have been injured some died, many more were widowed. The welfare of those who did return to Britain was left to the Commanding Officer or in the case of the navy, no-one at all. The women had to fend for themselves by any means available.

WHERE THERE ARE WOMEN, THERE are most often children. The fact that there would also have been a rabble of infants and youngsters of all ages accompanying the troops has often been overlooked. Some of these children worked for the troops and others just got into mischief in the way children often do, thieving, lighting fires, setting off alarms and causing a din.

Boys were of course seen as useful source of recruits. It has been documented in *The Army Children's Archives TACA* that a boy in India of five years old was signed up as a drummer boy. His father had been killed and engaging him appeared to be a way of ensuring he was fed and kept occupied. As a piece of extra information he went on to become Colour Sergeant John Murray who had a distinguished career as a soldier earning the Military Service Medal with 5 Bars and leaving the service with an injury aged 21 years. He had given 16 years' service.

In the Navy young boys aged around 10 years were regularly assigned as midshipman.

There was from around the 1600s an argument underway and much discussion in military circles concerning the provision of education both for the children of the regiment and also for the soldiers of senior non-commissioned ranks (SNCOs). Soldiers, recruited from the lower classes of society were often uneducated.

Children could not easily be protected from the misdeeds of some of the men around them who were often very rough in their ways. Commanding officers around this time started to interest themselves in the welfare of the children. This would have been partly for reasons of Christian philanthropy and partly to encourage the children and the low ranking men to read the Bible, thereby discouraging bad behaviour around camp.

The idea that children of the military were to be educated reached the ears of British civilians and was seen as a rather quaint idea. The homeland had not yet generally recognized any need to educate their own poor, it was just not a consideration that had previously arisen.

Possibly the first Army school was opened in Tangier. This outpost had come into the possession of Charles II as part of his dowry on his marriage to Catherine of Braganza and had therefore to be garrisoned. An entry in State Papers, dated 17th April, 1675 states:

We have thought fit to employ Richard Reynolds... of Our University of Cambridge in Our service as Schoolmaster in Tangier .

(Col. NT St. John Williams BA (1971); *Tommy Atkins' Children— The Story of the Education of the Army's Children 1675-1970*)

The school had been formed to deal with both boys and girls. It had the function of training the quarter-masters, armourers and craftsmen of all types who needed both literacy and numeracy to be efficient in their work. There was also the consideration that under fire, messages were usually sent in writing from officers to the NCOs further down the line. The soldiers' learning meant they were better equipped for their work as well as being better able to lead worthwhile, God-fearing lives.

A school in Poona, 1897; Royal Irish Rifles

As for the orphans produced by warfare and disease, boarding education was eventually developed to provide for them. Some of these schools are still in existence today.

CHAPTER 3

WATERLOO

WHAT'S IN A NAME?

IT IS WORTH SPENDING A chapter on Mavis at Waterloo since there is much written which tells some rather remarkable stories.

The women who had followed the Duke of Wellington's army had to cope with a great deal. There are descriptions of sad partings on the dawn of the battle and even sadder scenes when the news of a death reached the women who had stayed in Brussels away from the fighting. However, there were many who ventured onto the battle ground under fire.

Sergeant Major Henry Cotton, in his book *A Voice from Waterloo*, London, 1849, referring to the dead after the Battle of Waterloo:

'Many women were found amongst the slain... As is common in the camp, the camp followers wore male attire, with nearly as martial a bearing as the soldiers and some were even mounted and rode astride.'

It has been suggested that as many as 4,000 women, and of course children, accompanied the British Army at Waterloo 1815.

Although some did wear male clothing and actively fought, many of them were soldiers' families. They performed the function of ensuring their men were cared for when wounded. A similar number of *cantinieres* and *vivandieres* were with the French forces, again wearing something akin to a military uniform, and their function was acknowledged to be that of supplying cognac and sustenance to the French wounded following a battle.

Amongst the British, whole families would travel together. There are some heart-breaking stories of women who searched for their loved ones among the piles of dead soldiers left after the battle. It seems that the search for a loved one had especially momentous outcomes for some of the wives and for that reason their stories are well documented.

There follows detail of three births which took place immediately after the battle apparently as a result of the excitement and some very brave actions by the soldiers' wives.

The pregnant Margaret Tolmie did just that. She had accompanied her husband and also her father, both of the 2nd Royal North British Dragoons, Scots Greys, to Brussels where she and other women sat out the battle. On the day after the activities, she and the other ladies ventured out to find out what had become of their men. On the battlefield the wounded had been removed and all that remained was a mass of dead bodies. Margaret determinedly searched among the dead for her husband and eventually found him wounded and removed to some distance from where the battle had taken place. She persuaded two other women to carry him to where medical care could be given. The excitement of finding him alive caused her to give birth that very day.

Her story is not an isolated one. Ensign Thomas Deacon of the 73rd Foot was wounded. His pregnant wife Martha together with their three children spent a terrible night searching for him. The four of them walked twenty miles in a downpour to find him, thankfully alive, in Brussels. Once more this resulted in her giving birth to a baby girl whom they named Waterloo, a fine name to carry through life.

Private McMullen serving with the 27th Foot also had reason to be grateful to his courageous wife who while pregnant and at the height of the battle carried him off the battlefield when he had been shot in the knee. She became injured herself when a cannon ball fractured her leg and she proceeded to give birth to a baby girl there and then. The child, once again, was given the name Waterloo. The Duke of York and Albany became the child's proud godfather.

(Katherine Astbury – *Witnesses, Wives, Politicians, Soldiers: The women of Waterloo. The Conversation* June 12th 2015)

After the Battle of Waterloo

CHAPTER 4

ABSENT ON PARADE

NEW WAYS OF WAR

WITH THE COMING OF THE era of Napoleonic conflict the women who had always supported the military were about to be dealt a severe blow. One from which no-one gained. Much of the information in this chapter is taken from Myrna Trustram's book, **Women of the Regiment by Myrna Trustram** 2008.

Light Dragoon Barracks Room, 1788

Mavis was both a support and a drain on the Army. The women did need to be contained since as has been previously mentioned they were known to be avid scavengers and looters. Although an invaluable asset for many years the Army chose at this time in the mid 19th century to reduce its reliance on families. The consequences were rather unfortunate.

The French Revolution and Napoleonic Wars meant European conflicts were beginning to be organized differently. Armies became larger and the public were becoming concerned with the cost of keeping them operational since military actions were more visible, due to greater media coverage. It was felt armies needed to function in a more controlled, professional manner.

The belief at the War Office and the Admiralty was that a soldier's 'family' should be the regiment in which he served, or for the sailor's the ship on which he was a member of the crew. Where Mavis may have been a licensed or un-licensed sutler, laundress, nurse or cook she would now be replaced by a soldier who would provide the same very necessary services to his fellow soldiers.

A misguided view prevailed that most women attached to the army were of bad character and an unnecessary drain on resources. This was an incorrect over simplified view and as ever those in high places tended to make moral judgements, often untrue, that they would not apply to themselves. Married soldiers, were considered a burden.

With this in mind the generals, admirals and war politicians, would naturally prefer to have an army of free, single men unencumbered by family duties and ties. Mavis, it was believed, could be dispensed with completely. There was no need for camp-following women, wives or self-employed women to assist the soldiers with domestic needs.

It was considered that a deterrent was needed to prevent men from marrying. Thus soldiers and sailors were required to ask the permission of their Commanding Officer before marrying. (This rule was still in force in the 1990s, though often ignored.) Such permission was not at that time expected to be granted.

That the work force should be made up of 'celibate bachelors' was an incredibly short sighted view and demonstrates how little credit had been given to the work the women previously undertook. Also, there was no desire to spend money from the War Chest on providing for families.

Most men undoubtedly wanted to support their wives and families but this was not made easy. They were often separated from their loved ones by being posted overseas, where they might be killed in battle. A few soldiers, and there will always be some, were glad to shed their family responsibilities. The recruiting officers gleefully advertised this aspect of the job as a prime advantage to joining up:

> 'Join the Army and we shall make it a place of refuge for you from your liability to maintain your wife and children.'

In the new army Commanding Officers would not have been encouraged to take an interest in the plight of the soldiers' families. This was not the prevailing culture. However, confining young men to barracks and expecting them to forsake the outside world was obviously extremely short-sighted and a premise born of ignorance. It did not work of course. No force could succeed in eliminating the desire, of most soldiers, for sex, family life and the presence of women and children.

At this time Mavis may have become an unacknowledged wife or even a loose woman. The men could not now easily marry. Women in many roles would be present outside the barrack gates or port entrances. Thus the new thinking had the opposite effect on the moral behaviour and efficiency of the men in the military. Now, laying with prostitutes and drinking became the preferred activity chosen by many, many more soldiers and sailors than had previously been the case.

It was generally accepted that there existed within this group of men:

'The innate sexual passion of soldiers which need an outlet.'

The men would need to be passionate and virile to do the job of soldiering. The authorities were loath to allow them to waste all that pent up energy on women. There was an acknowledgement that as the men drank and whored, the result was a very unhealthy army. However the problem was definitely seen to be the fault of the women.

An extract from an Army Medical Report dated 1859 comments on the appalling number of men requiring hospital treatment primarily for venereal disease. These are the noted admissions to hospital annually per 1,000 men within each of the following regiments—

	1859	1837-46
Household Cavalry	120.4	
Dragoon Guards and Dragoons	402.5	206.1
Royal Artillery	571.4	392
Royal Engineers	468.2	
Military Train	580.3	
Foot Guards	337.9	250.3
Infantry Regiments	399.4	277.5
Depot Battalions	399.8	

This is but a sample, the list goes on. Nearly half the army were treated for venereal disease at some time.

The Household Cavalry had a lower number of casualties (120 per 1,000) which was attributed to there being a larger number of married men in that section.

The problem was seriously concerning to those in government. The War Office and Admiralty appointed a committee under Samuel Whitbread to write a report which concluded as follows. The committee—

> '…feel it is a duty to press on the government the necessity of at once grappling with the mass of vice, filth, and disease which surrounds the soldiers' barracks and the seamen's homes, which not only crowds our hospitals, it weakens the roll of effectiveness…saps the vigour of our soldiers and seamen, sows the seeds of degradation and degeneracy…'

Florence Nightingale was involved with the committee and was pleased to note a suggestion put forward to divert these passionate and virile men:

'Soldiers should be encouraged in some form of handicraft to occupy their time in barracks.'

This was followed by the more practical one:

'A greater number should be encouraged to marry.'

Needless to say the handicrafts idea did not solve the problem and the blame for the increase in diseases was still seen to rest firmly with the women. The 1864 and 1866 Contagious Diseases Acts were passed. They stated that a policeman could put before a magistrate his suspicions that a woman was a prostitute and diseased. If after a compulsory medical examination she was found to be infected she could be detained in hospital for up to three months. A system of registration and fortnightly examination was introduced. Non-compliance led to imprisonment for up to six months.

A policeman of that era, poorly paid and not necessarily gifted with great intellect, could therefore arrest any woman he chose and his judgement would be final. Thus no account was taken of the number of innocent women who underwent this humiliating and degrading procedure and were completely free of any disease, and on occasion had been going about their daily business, not even having been with a man. The system of inspecting prostitutes was felt to be a necessary procedure in all port and garrison areas, of which there were many.

There was a clear understanding that having a wife would reduce the problem, but current thinking favoured the idea that marriage was incompatible with a sailor's or soldier's life.

There were some limited sanctions imposed, to discourage the men from having sex and becoming ill. It was ordered that they should be docked 10 old pence from their pay for the duration of any of their stays in hospital.

Unsurprisingly none of these measures was successful. The National Anti-Contagious Diseases Association was formed with considerable national support and eventually the acts were repealed after a twenty year period in 1886.

CHAPTER 5

WHAT FAMILY?

HARD TIMES, LIMITED ACTION

AS A RESULT OF THIS worrying situation there were movements in Parliament towards providing for wives and enabling certain long serving men to have wives in the billets with them. Officers of course had always been permitted to have their wives accompany them on their postings so long as it was at their own expense.

It was argued that allowing some long-serving members of the rank and file to have their wives with them could solve part of the problem of the men's unhealthy lifestyles and would also give an incentive to some men to make a long term career of being a soldier.

The arrangements for families took many years to work out. In the mid 1800s for the first time the number of wives officially permitted to be 'on the strength' was specified. There was an allowance for their food and they were officially permitted to live in barracks. When the regiment moved on to another place, the travelling expenses of the wife and family were paid. The allowance went to the chosen soldiers as follows:

All regimental staff sergeants,

60% of other sergeants,

7% of ranks where the man had served 7 years and was in possession of a good conduct badge.

Both the man and his wife had to be of good conduct or the privilege would be removed.

Photos from *TACA (The Army Children's Archives)* show the soldiers' families, most notably corporals and above, often sporting good conduct stripes. They show some rather glum looking families but that was probably due to the conditions needed for a good photo. There are reports of families enjoying themselves at picnics, sports days and children's parties.

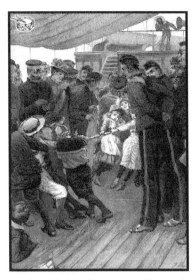

Children's Tug of War on a homeward bound troop ship—
boys versus girls

Queen Victoria seems to have been aware that the men valued their families and also of the challenges facing military wives. This can be seen in the illustration by S. Begg:

Her Majesty Addressing the Wives and Children of The Household
Cavalry and Reservists at Windsor

Were Mavis a sergeant's wife she would have been an experienced campaigner, better able to keep herself and her man alive and on the right side of the Commanding Officer. For this same reason were she to become widowed she would be likely to be in demand as a wife for a young newly recruited private.

If she were a wife 'on the strength' there was still no payment to her if her husband died, other than in action. Without her soldier husband Mavis would doubtless be destitute and without support.

To deal with this eventuality it has been suggested that an ancient custom within the army at the time of a wedding required the groom to name his closest friend as the 'Best Man'. The duty of this chosen comrade would be to take on the bridegroom's wife should he be killed or die of disease. This would especially be the case if that worst case scenario occurred in some foreign land. There is no record of whether this arrangement worked or not.

Once again the solution was not ideal. Mavis may have been allowed to join her husband 'on the strength', to live in the barracks or married quarters. There remained a large number of men who kept wives and girlfriends outside the garrison 'off the strength'. Mavis may have become a sad abandoned or impoverished wife through no fault of her own, or of her man either.

Married Without Leave, Left behind on the Departure of the Regiment

Since women were no longer being paid for the work they did and since Poor Relief was no longer provided for soldiers or sailor's families, there was increased hardship for military unrecognised families. As Myrna Trustram informs us in Women of the Regiment 1980:

'On marriage the mobile lifestyle of a soldier meant a woman had effectively given up her family and neighbourhood ties. Soldiers during a fifteen year engagement could be expected to spend five years in Britain and ten years abroad. The 93rd Regiment spent 23 years in India from 1847-1870.'

The new Poor Law Amendment Acts 1834, 1873, excluded any provision for military wives. It is easy to see how women ended up alone, having no support. Wives no longer qualified for 'outdoor relief', that is money to support themselves within a community. Poor Law Guardians, in port or garrison towns, showed an unwillingness to pay for the expenses of military families who were not and never had been members of their community.

That left the Workhouse as the only remaining option for these poor, abandoned, families who being able-bodied did not qualify anyway. Conditions were pretty unacceptable in the workhouse where there was segregation of families and a very poor existence. No one would willingly enter the Workhouse unless they were desperate. A wife 'off the strength' was effectively forgotten by the society.

The following is an extract of a poem written in 1899 by Rudyard Kipling, penned specifically to raise money for the wives and children of soldiers who fought in the 2nd Boer War.

The Absent Minded Beggar

'But we do not want his kiddies to remind him

That we sent 'em to the workhouse

While their daddy hammered Paul,

So we'll help the homes that Tommy left behind him!'

Moving as a wife 'off the strength', within Britain, would entail considerable cost. It could be prohibitive for the man to finance a move of home and support the family. A report from Colchester illustrates this point:

'After stoppages to pay for their families' travel from Ireland to Colchester, men off the married strength had little more than a penny a day to support their families.'

Mavis may have successfully obtained work in whatever area she found herself or she may not. However there could have been difficulties which were reported by a group of wives in Colchester 1856-7.

'Work for the wives was harder to find in Colchester than it had been in Ireland and fuel and lodging were more expensive.'

This was the situation at Colchester Barracks where there were:

'more than 250 wives and 350 children living in squalor with no fire, no blankets and hardly any food.'

The intervention of **Major (later Colonel) Sir James Gildea**, an officer of the Royal Warwickshire Regiment, was particularly timely. He wrote a letter to the *Times* 1885 which pricked the nation's conscience.

Colonel Gildea had already raised money for the support of military dependants in the Zulu, Afghan and the Indian conflicts by setting up an administration to give aid to dependants both on and off the strength. He organised middle class and well-to-do women in committees in garrison and port towns throughout Britain to undertake this work.

Having been actively involved in aiding the Queen to set up her '**Queen Victoria's Jubilee Institute for Nurses**', he saw the value of having trained nurses in areas where there were large numbers of military families. To this end in 1892 he inaugurated a nursing service to provide fully qualified District Nurses to tend to military families, most often those 'off the strength'.

Mrs **Norah Diamond** was the first nurse employed in 1892 by **SSFA 'Soldiers and Sailors Families Association'** the organisation set up by Colonel Gildea. She was a devoted, hard working heroine of a woman, employed at Curragh Camp in Dublin, and her terms of employment required her to:

> '…walk some distance in her day's work and make shift with the minimum of conveniences.'

She was paid £70 per year plus 18 shillings per month for fuel in winter and 9 shillings in summer. Her hut was rent free. We are told her hut may not have been a great deal better than the 'hovels not fit for animals' that the families lived in.

> 'In her first two months Mrs Diamond made 300 visits in which nursing care was required plus many more giving advice. The following year her total nursing visits rose to 2,226 plus friendly visits… After living for 5 years in her hut, she was cheered to realise that at a Garden Fete in the grounds of Chelsea Hospital the magnificent sum of £1,093 was raised to build her a house at Curroch Camp Ireland.

> (*Alison Barnes; The History of SSAFA, Part 1: The Early Years.*)

She served for 30 years, retiring in 1922.

By 1897 there were 12 such nurses and the service grew to include care for families returning from abroad. These families were in a dire situation coming from war torn areas to a place they did not know at all. Once more his committees in port areas were able to provide food and shelter for the returnees.

For officers' widows and orphans, a home was built in Wimbledon, London, opened by the Princess of Wales, later to become Queen Alexandra, who was a real supporter of the organisation, always ready to help with fund raising. **Queen Alexandra** who gave her name to the **Queen Alexandra Nursing Corpse,** became the first president of **SSFA** now called **SSAFA** to include the Royal Air Force.

CHAPTER 6

A SPY?

OR POSSIBLY NOT—NAMED WOMEN 1900-1918

POSSIBLY THE ATTRIBUTES AND SITUATIONS of a good spy are more mundane than those portrayed by James Bond. A recent *Times* interview with a MI6 operative who gave her name as Lisa, quoted her as saying that women made the best spies:

> '…they have an enhanced ability to multi-task and are good at tapping into different emotional resources.'

Be that as it may, it takes a particular type of woman to be prepared to sacrifice her freedom, family and sometimes her life to gather information in dangerous situations.

The information used in this and the next chapters comes from Dr Vivien Newman's book **We Also Served** 2014, also The Imperial War Museum, London, and other sources. It is necessary to mention one or two women who were probably not spies but left the impression that they were. In the first instance there was **Mata Hari**, an exotic dancer during World War 1, who entertained the German troops in Paris. She probably did not give information to the Germans and is now not thought to have been a spy although she did, unwisely, accept money from the Germans in occupation. This caused her to be executed in October 1917.

Another less notorious dancer, a Swiss named **Regina Diane**, suffered a similar fate. Possibly exotic dancers had opportunities not open to others and the public was only too willing to see them as 'up to no good'.

Dame Edith Cavell as a nurse was in an excellent position to gather information which helped over 200 allied soldiers escape from Belgium. She nursed and saved the lives of both Allied and German soldiers and gained the trust and considerable respect from both sides. This did not prevent her being executed by the Germans in October 1915.

Next I give three examples of female spies who worked for Britain in Belgium during World War I. All were betrayed to the Germans. Two were executed and one imprisoned.

Gabrielle Petit is still considered a hero in Belgium having worked for two years for the British Secret Service. Her spying career started when she was working for the Belgian Red Cross and she smuggled her injured fiancé, a soldier, across the Dutch border to join allied forces. She subsequently smuggled further soldiers to safety and in the process gained valuable information about the movements of the Kaiser's Army. The British Secret Service realised her value and gave her training in intelligence techniques in 1915.

Although she never gave secrets away she had confided some of her work to an undercover German agent who was posing as a Dutchman. She was 23 when she was executed by the Germans in 1916.

Elise Grandprez, also Belgian, served as a supervisor, train watcher, courier and most impressively she transcribed reports she obtained in invisible ink which she used to write onto ordinary wrappings which were carried to the Chief of Intelligence in Liege. Together with members of her family and other contacts she was successful until their contact was caught by the Germans and shot. A year later in 1917 most of her network were caught and imprisoned. Elise and Constance Granprez and Andre Gregoire were condemned to death and shot in 1917.

Martha Crockaert was highly honoured for her espionage work for Britain, France and Belgium. She was also awarded the Iron Cross by Germany for her nursing services.

Her home in West Flanders had been razed to the ground by the Germans August 1914. As a trained nurse and a linguist she gained a job at a German Military Hospital in the village.

Working as a nurse, in a hospital near enemy lines, which treated those from both sides of the conflict, she used the codename *Laura*. She was able to pass information, to her Anglo Belgian espionage contacts for two years. There were two other female spies with whom she worked, an elderly vegetable seller codenamed *Canteen Ma* and a letterbox agent codenamed *Number 63*.

Her lodger Otto, recruited her to become an agent for the other side and spy for the Germans. After sending a few useless messages she found the work of a double agent too difficult. She arranged to have Otto killed.

Her exploits for Britain included destroying a telephone line used by a local priest who was spying for the Germans and she also attempted to blow up a German ammunition dump from a disused sewer. That operation led to her exposure. She was captured and sentenced to death.

Her sentence was commuted to imprisonment due to her having been awarded the Iron Cross for her nursing services to the Germans. She was released when the Armistice came and she married John McKenna and became a writer. She managed to arrange for Sir Winston Churchill to write a foreword to her memoire, *I was a Spy* which she wrote under her married name.

Gertrude Bell was in a class of her own, slim, neat and with thick wavy hair she tended to lend any fraught diplomatic situation an air of calm. Working for the British government on the diplomatic front in the Middle East, she has directly influenced our world today.

She started her life in the Middle East as an archaeologist and mountaineer and made good relationships with many of the Arab tribes during the early 1900s. In following these activities she gained considerable respect and was enabled to '*move as an equal amongst the sheikhs*'.

Gertrude Bell

At that time the dismantling of the Ottoman Empire was taking place. She became known in the British diplomatic service for her intimate knowledge and understanding of the Middle East and what was taking place in political circles. It was for this reason she was eventually employed to assess the situation there.

She became involved in setting the borders for a newly-defined Iraq, formerly known as Mesopotamia. Her use to the British government was as a mediator between the various factions who were constantly at war, Sunnis and Shias, and Kurds. She guided T.E Lawrence (Lawrence of Arabia) in much of his work and became an integral part of the administration of

Iraq. As a *Guardian* article Wednesday 12th March 2003 reported:

'Miss Bell is still a name in Baghdad'.

'And in Baghdad in 1921 she drew the boundaries of the country that became Iraq'.

She never married although she had a close relationship with a married man who was killed at Gallipoli in 1915.

THE BEGINNING OF THE TWENTIETH century brought more of the details of war to public notice. There were more magazine articles, more letters available and with the birth of the Suffragette movement there was generally more interest in the activities of remarkable women. Many of these women, but not all, were high born and privileged. This does not diminish the daring deeds of the more privileged, they just had more opportunities, which they took.

Dorothy Lawrence, born 1884, was not privileged nor was she a spy. Her parentage is unknown and she was adopted by a Church of England Guardian who sexually abused her as a child. She had published short pieces in the *Times* before 1914 but wanted to be a fully fledged journalist and report on life in the trenches during the war against Germany's Kaiser. To this end she travelled to France.

Believing that it was the only way she would obtain her story she flattened her chest, removed and hid her petticoats and eventually persuaded a group of young royal engineers, her *'Khaki Accomplices'*, to provide her with male clothing. Tom Dunn a young, ex-coalmining sapper, assisted her. He feared for her safety amongst the sex hungry men and found her a damp, disused cottage in Senilis Forest where she slept at night. He assisted her to gain work with the 179 tunnelling division of the 51st Division of the Royal Engineers. She travelled throughout the trenches masquerading as a man and gained access to some personal stories that the War Office would not permit to be published until after the Armistice.

Unfortunately Dorothy became ill in France. As a result of this and fearing she would faint and be discovered in circumstances beyond her control, she chose to hand herself into the authorities where she came to the notice of Sir Walter Kirke of the British Expeditionary Forces secret service. Maybe she was genuinely thought to be a spy or perhaps those in power were fearful that she would publish her news report or discredit the Army by just being there. Either way she became a prisoner of war.

Her written account of the fuss her behaviour caused is most entertaining. She was a diminutive young woman who once her gender was exposed, saw no reason to continue wearing male clothing. So wearing her petticoats, which made her look extremely feminine she was taken by horseback to the Third Army Headquarters in Calais. There she was interrogated somewhat excessively by six Generals and twenty other officers. She let them know how foolish she thought they all were and how she felt their treatment of her was well over the top and quite unnecessary.

The Army was embarrassed by their breach of security and were fearful that once her guise was disclosed other women would take on the same sort of expedition. On the orders of a suspicious judge she was committed to a convent and effectively silenced.

On her return to Britain she met Emmeline Pankhurst and agreed to give a talk about her experiences. The War Office became heavily involved. She was forbidden to give the talk or to publish her story and forced to sign an affidavit agreeing not to publish or speak of her experiences at all.

Sadly after the armistice in 1919 no one in war weary Britain was interested in her or her writings. She wrote her book but made no money and lapsed into mental ill health.

Flora Sandes is another woman who was in a class of her own, born January 1876 into a middle class family in Marlesford, Suffolk, she had always wished she had been born a boy. In her teens she already spoke several languages, had trained in First Aid and learnt to drive. These were ideal attributes for women in the newly formed First Aid Nursing Yeomanry F.A.N.Ys which offered volunteer nursing, first aid and driving services. She had the further attribute of being a good shot with a rifle and service revolver and could drink 'like a trooper'. After several trial attempts it was found that she just did not fit the 'Angel of Mercy' image that was attached to the medical units which were springing up to aid the wounded. She was subsequently given short shrift by all the matrons of the newly formed, well disciplined front line casualty units that she sampled.

Going further afield she joined the service of Britain's ally Serbia. She was welcomed by the Serb/American Red Cross Unit which had been formed by the wife of the Serbian Secretary of State for Foreign Affairs, Mabel Grouitch. During the Unit's three week journey to the Balkans, she behaved in a manner that suited her true personality: wallets and reputations were lost, never to be found again. Flora was known to have warmed the beds of a number of fellow travellers, male and female.

Working in a typhus ridden hospital in Valjevo, in an unqualified capacity, Flora proved herself a competent nurse, anaesthetist and even surgeon. She had been forced to take on the surgeon's role since the professional staff had succumbed to typhoid. Indeed she did eventually become ill with the disease herself, but she managed to survive. Twenty-one of the doctors died and many nurses.

At the fall of Belgrade, October 1915, Flora decided to travel nearer to the front line as a member of the Serbian Field

Ambulance Unit. She enrolled as a woman, in the 2nd Regiment of the 1st Serbian Army, the only British woman to do so. Handling herself very effectively as a soldier, when necessary with the use of her service revolver she became very popular.

On a number of occasions she was seriously near death, for example at the 41st British Military Hospital for Serbian soldiers she was very ill with influenza. Finding the treatment she was given by the medical staff at the hospital was not effective, she chose to treat herself with horse linctus, which clearly did the trick.

She rose through the ranks, always as a woman, eventually gaining a commission to the rank of captain. Her disguise must have been absolutely convincing, as she was accused by a prostitute of fathering a child.

Flora Sandes

Back in Britain an Act of Parliament was needed to enable her to be recognized as captain within her home shore. As a respected member of Britain's ally Serbia, it was felt her rank should receive due recognition. Although Suffolk born, it was felt that in order for her commission to be recognised in Britain she had to be defined as a foreigner by Parliament. A special Act was passed for this purpose. She was said to be a Serbian since it was the only way a British female commissioned officer could be tolerated and openly acknowledged. She was awarded 15 medals, one of which was the 'Kara George Star' the highest honour that could be given by Serbia.

After the war Flora lived with her Russian husband Yuri Yudenitch in Belgrade where she became the city's first female taxi driver. In a letter to a friend she spoke of a hat she had been persuaded to buy because she was *'a lady again'* and of her longing for the *'…action-packed days and vodka-soaked nights'* of her days in the Serbian Army.

CHAPTER 7

NO PETTICOATS HERE

EARLY NURSING SERVICES, 1900-1919

AT THE BEGINNING OF THE 1900s the official medical services at the front line were manned by soldiers with their main function being to get men back to the front lines as soon as possible. Care was rudimentary to say the least, situations were insanitary and many men died in horrible conditions.

Because of the need not only to preserve man power but to reduce avoidable suffering Mavis was beginning to gain some recognition. There were a few female doctors, nurses, ambulance drivers and mechanics making the journey to give service in the various war zones. There were many women who just did what they could.

Inhabitants Evacuated from Marne—Friends House

Dr. Vivien Newman in her book **We Also Served** (2014) gives an account of the way thousands of women contributed their aid to the war effort, sometimes with little encouragement.

Certainly the presence of Mavis is recorded in the Anglo-Zulu War, the Boer War and later in the Balkans. In the early years most women were volunteers from well to do families or working for self-funding organisations. Gallingly they had to face the injustice of the male orderlies working alongside them being paid.

By the beginning of the First World War nearly 2,000 Commonwealth and British trained nurses had already given service. Nearly 1,000 of those early pioneers had come from Canada, New Zealand and Australia.

Australian nurses were in the majority and during the First World War, 2,562 of them took a leap in the dark and travelled from their homeland not knowing where they would be sent to work.

Altogether 24,000 professional nurses plus numerous orderlies cared for 637,746 patients needing care as a result of wartime activities.

F.A.N.Y., the **First Aid Nursing Yeomanry** and **Mrs Mabel St. Claire Stobart's Wounded Convoy Corps** formed in the early 1900s were well established by 1914. Funding themselves and raising money at home they saved many lives by collecting the injured from the battle areas and driving them in horse drawn or motorised ambulances to Treatment Centres where there was medical help.

There were many more groups becoming established, all working without pay, government support or recognition to ease the suffering of the men.

Among these groups were the women of the **Voluntary Aid Detachment (V.A.D.)** who from their own pockets needed to find £1.19d for a uniform before they were able to start working. Another was **Evalena Haverfield's Women's Emergency**

Corp who provided feeding centres for soldiers and refugees. There were also the **Women's Volunteer Reserves, Mrs Dawson's Defence Relief Corps**, the **Red Cross** and **St John's Ambulance Brigade** all doing similar work.

Many women signed up as nurses with the **Friends Ambulance Units** (FAU) a Quaker organisation of over 1,500 Conscientious Objectors who in common with most of the other voluntary groups treated people of both sides in the conflict.

FAU—Hospital Staff, Dunkirk 1914—Friends House

Some of the Units mentioned above, though willing to treat all comers, felt the need to keep the two sides in separate areas. This was both to avoid conflict amongst the non-ambulant and to protect information, since loose tongues could cause dangerous situations to develop.

THE EXISTING FIRST AID UNITS offered their services freely to the War Office but were not officially acknowledged as having any useful purpose. When **Dr Elsie Inglis** of the **Scottish Women's Hospitals** was offered an audience at the War Office August 1914 she was told :

'My good lady, go home and sit still—no petticoats here.'

A branch of the **First Aid Nursing Yeomanry F.A.N.Y. Corp**, not deterred, made arrangements to cross the channel with the Belgian Army and six women left for France 27th October 1914. There were three nurses, two orderlies, a doctor and £12 of Corps funds in the bank. They had arranged for friends to send sheets and provisions later and on arrival moved to set up a field hospital in the almost derelict and disused Lamark Convent School, Paris. The school was dirty and smelt of the outside latrines. On their arrival the women encountered forty desperately ill men lying on plank beds inside. One consolation was that the east window of Notra Dame Cathedral faced their yard.

With help from the **British Red Cross**, Lamark Hospital soon had 100 good beds and by 1916 had treated more than 4,000 patients driven to the hospital by **FANY** drivers.

Before long **FANY** was running more field hospitals. Apart from offering medical help the women were driving and maintaining ambulances, operating a motor bath providing 250 baths a day and disinfecting the soldiers' clothes.

They also set up soup kitchens and field canteens in dangerous situations along the Western Front. All this could be achieved with just **120 FANYs**. This gallant group had, by the Armistice between them been awarded:

17 British Military Medals,

1 Legion d'Honneur

27 Croix de Guerre.

A rather amazing group of women worked with the aristocratic **Millicent, Duchess of Sutherland**, who had no time for the Army's *'this is men's work'*, attitude. As has been mentioned before, the Army seriously attempted to prevent women from travelling into what was seen as their male domain. Using her contacts and supplied by friends Millicent Sutherland formed an

Ambulance Unit and was able go ahead of the British Expeditionary Force to France where she was able to bypass the authorities. She offered her fully equipped Unit to the grateful Belgians.

The account of their exploits amongst both the Allies and the Germans is given in a diary account by one of her nurses, **Florence Ford** who documented it in *Six Weeks at the War*. The group were situated in a convent near Namur which was under constant bombardment. Florence wondered what was worse:

'...being shelled or knowing that you were hemmed in by fires'

She relates what transpired once Paris fell to the Germans and their little unit was in German territory:

'Once Namur fell, and with over 100 patients in her care,
Millicent set about harrying the German Commander, whom she
visited daily, in order to bother him and quote the Convention of
Geneva...to lighten the load of our wounded.'

Florence reported that Millicent whom she considered '*most brave*', had confided that the German Commander of Namur must have been:

'...getting sick of me and my ambulance unit'.

Millicent managed to avoid her patients being transported to Germany and in exasperation, it seems, the Commander agreed for them to be sent on a German train to what was seen as a safer area. It was actually an area that had surrendered two days earlier to the Germans.

They crossed the battlefield and saw the tanks and the trenches. The women and probably the patients were subsequently sent to Brussels where they were all imprisoned in the Hotel Asturias. Kate felt this was '*...a jolly good hotel*' where they all especially appreciated the luxury of being served a meal of poached eggs and buttered toast. In the meantime Millicent was busy breaking the protocol concerning proper behaviour of a lady:

> '…interviewing every person of distinction. She really is quite splendid & and it is quite the usual thing to receive visitors in one's bedroom.'

The German Military Governor of Brussels was one of her guests and he duly succumbed to her persuasion and gave permission for the group to return to Britain.

A much needed quality amongst women independently setting up a hospital in war torn Europe was determination. It is an attribute often directed towards **Dr Elsie Inglis**. She not only qualified as a doctor but with her team and her equipment, which had been donated, she managed to travel to war torn Serbia.

When the Russian Revolution made the work of her unit impossible she held up the Revolution by a day in order to get her equipment safely back to Britain. This came about because her unit needed to board a boat for England at Archangel before the encroaching winter set in. She insisted her equipment which had been donated by the good folk in Britain, was also loaded onto the ship.

In order for this to happen she managed to break a strike called by Trotsky and the Bolsheviks. It seems the strikers preferred to break the Trotsky's strike than face her wrath. Throughout her expedition she had been aware that she was suffering from terminal cancer so probably she felt she had nothing to lose.

CHAPTER 8

A TRAY OF DRESSINGS AND A PAIL

RECOGNITION OF THE NEED FOR NURSES

WE ALL KNOW THE ARMY loves Three Letter Abbreviations (TLAs). Apart from the Casualty Clearing Stations (CCS) and Base Hospitals there were also 12 Ambulance Trains (ATs), 7 Hospital Ships (HMHS) and Barges.

The nurses and other female workers in the last chapter were mostly volunteers but in her role as a volunteer Mavis had shown herself to be invaluable. As the war progressed the volunteers were joined by the **Queen Alexandra Nurses** and others who were in the employ of the military. I shall not differentiate between the two groups. They all had the same objective of treating the wounded and transporting men to where they could receive further care.

Kate Luard, a veteran of the Boer War, had an excellent reputation for the high standard of cheerfulness and cleanliness amongst the men at her Frontline Clearing Station. This was helped in part by the supplies she persuaded her friends and family to send from back home in Witham, Essex. The men with head injuries had '*bright, soft cushions*' to lie on and there were many other little luxuries.

Kate eventually found herself posted onto an Ambulance Train. It was a role she had looked forward to undertaking but as a Train Sister the demands were enormous. They were required to take as many as 510 men on a train, '*miles long*', from the front line to the coast for transportation to the UK. In the early part of the war conditions for the Sisters were hard to believe. Most of the men's dressings were old, most had lice and many wounds were gangrenous.

> '…nurses made tea in cans using the engine's water…you boarded a cattle truck armed with a tray of dressings and a pail.'

At the beginning of the War the trains had no corridors and although prohibited from doing so, nurses clambered from coach to coach using the footboards while the train was in motion, carrying:

> '…a load on their backs. The load was a bag, as aseptic as possible…which contained dressings, medicaments and at night when going from one coach to another, the Sisters had to carry hurricane lamps suspended from their arms.'

There were no facilities for the Sisters who lived on the trains. Every so often they would stop at a station and attempt to have a wash, still cleaning their teeth while clambering back on the train.

Shortly before Christmas 1914 the situation of the nurses came to the ear of Queen Alexandra who graciously sent them a Christmas present of tea and sweets, most welcome. Eventually situations improved when trains with corridors came into being making life so much easier.

Hospital Ships and Hospital Barges presented their own particular challenges. Where possible the patients who needed to be kept relatively still were transported across France by canal on a flotilla of barges. These were often reported as cheerful places, favoured by many nurses and patients. The British media had a soft spot for them too.

Because the barges had become a target for the German fighter pilots (their prominent Red Crosses, the symbol of neutrality, were seen as a target), the nurses who regularly worked 15 hour shifts had to do their night rounds on slippery decks, in the dark using small torches to avoid giving the enemy something to aim at.

As always the nurses were forever begging for comforts from home. Letters reached home asking for such things as the cleaner VIM, or a 'pudding recipe', since the diet on board had become seriously monotonous and keeping the place well scrubbed was always a problem.

The Hospital Ships (HMHS) operated on the Western front bringing greater numbers of men back to England. At first there was little action and some of the nurses wrote letters home in which they spoke of their pleasant situation sunning themselves aboard ship. The holiday environment did not last.

A report from Anna Cameron serving aboard HMS Delta described how their ship was moored off Gallipoli, 1915, within sound and range of the guns, which the Turks were firing at them. Miraculously only one of their ships was hit and the nurses watched it go down while waiting for the queue of casualties to come pouring on board from the battlefield.

'We had taken 400 horribly wounded men straight from the field. One needed all ones common sense and courage…They came pouring in. We three sisters had 200 of the wounded and only 6 orderlies, so many (orderlies) were needed for stretcher bearers…we wrapped them (the men) in their filthy clothes and let them rest… Faces shot away, arms, legs, lungs, shot everywhere. One (of the wounded) said "Thank God We Have the Sisters".'

The Casualty Clearing stations at the front line of battle zones were every bit as harrowing since they also had to contend with treating awfully wounded men while also being in the line of fire.

Elsie Grant, Belgium 1917, explains to a friend:

'We have been up in Belgium at the 3rd Australian Casualty Clearing Station. We have been shelled out three times but this last time was too dreadful…one sister killed and one wounded. Our hospital is a total wreck now…we can hear guns quite plainly…shells were whistling, there was a dreadful explosion and everything was lighted up…the wounded (began) pouring in.'

Another Elsie, an Australian, Elsie Tranter in May 1917 reported that she:

'…had to assist at 10 amputations one after another. It is frightfully nerve-racking work and I seem to hear the wretched saw every time I try to sleep.'

Poisonous gas in the trenches was also a hazard that physically and mentally affected the nurses:

'Those of us who are working amongst the gassed men have lost our voices and can just about manage to whisper.'

Nurses were issued with gas masks which were put to a number of uses not originally intended. Though pretty useless for protecting against gas they made excellent pillows. In fact unbeknownst to the issuing authorities, the best protection against the effect of the gas the men were bringing with them were found to be **Dr Southall's Hygienic Towels for Women**. Tin hats were also issued and it seems the nurses tended when under fire to sleep with them over their stomachs—clearly the part they wanted most to protect.

CHAPTER 9

HOME FIRES

WHAT JOBS DIDN'T WOMEN DO?

THROUGHOUT HISTORY WOMEN HAVE BY necessity, circumstance or choice been involved in many wartime activities. Lower class women had always taken on whatever work was available. It was inevitable that such women were unseen and not given a consideration.

Before 1914 there had been no thought amongst the upper classes that women were capable of doing the same work as men. When upper class women had chosen a career, the attitude was that of bewilderment. They were thought to be unnatural.

There were very occasionally female doctors and fortunately **Florence Nightingale** had ensured nursing could conceivably be considered a suitable profession for well bred ladies as it could have been seen as a continuation of the domestic role women were expected to take. Certainly women drivers and car mechanics would have caused quite a stir.

The coming of the First World War (1914-1918) coincided with the formation of the Suffragette movement and women's demands for a vote. Though women's demands for some form of equality were considered a real nuisance by most parliamentarians, a distraction, it was becoming increasingly clear to some that women could be useful to the War effort.

In early 1914 a use was found for some rather keen, rather young women who wanted involvement in the war at any cost.

It was apparent that there was a critical need for men to volunteer for war service. Some women had a romantic notion that a man was attractive if he was in uniform, willing to fight for his country. This was not lost on the **Parliamentary Recruiting Committee**.

They decided that young girls were to encourage their men folk to sign up for active service by appealing to the men's virility. The *Daily Mail* took to the cause with relish and we are pretty familiar with the posters issued by the **White Feather Movement**:

> 'Women of Britain Say Go' & 'Why Is Your Best Boy not in Khaki?'

'White Feather Girls' would roam the streets with enthusiasm to pin a white feather on any man not in uniform with the intention of naming him as a coward and shaming him into enlisting. The fact that these actions caused distress to all manner of men was not considered.

Sadly these girls gave no thought to the men, not always in uniform, who would be working in jobs important to the war effort. There was no thought given to the men who would have felt it immoral to go to war to kill someone but would prefer another occupation of value to the nation, sometimes an incredibly dangerous one as in the case of ambulance drivers and bomb disposal experts. There were also those who would prefer to be shunned by society and imprisoned as Conscientious Objectors, hardly cowards.

To encourage men to feel ever more gallant the idea was suggested that if Germany gained a foothold in Britain no woman would be safe. Men were urged to enlist to protect

British women from the hoards of invading 'Huns'. Press coverage spoke of 'The Rape of Belgium' accompanied by accounts of suitable lurid atrocities committed against women in enemy occupied countries.

There were a number of approaches to the war among the female population and much puzzlement amongst feminists. Before WWI the **Women's Suffrage Societies** had been united in their opposition to military action. However once war was a reality most women felt the need to knuckle down and try, as ever, to reduce the suffering of the victims of war both at home and overseas. This caused a rift in the Suffragette movement.

As THE WAR PROGRESSED IT became imperative to increase the military man power. Mavis was needed to fill posts at home so the men could be freed to go to war. The idea of paid work, certainly more than could be earned 'in service', appealed to many women who up to that point had had little choice of employment. When it was stated that able bodied women were needed to register for work 20,000 did so within the first weeks. 1.6 million women were recorded as having joined the workforce by the end of the war.

Mavis could have been a post lady, tram driver, tractor driver, bus conductor, boot maker, mechanic, police woman, fire woman, clerk and of course a woman working in a munitions factory or on a farm as a land girl. There were even women pilots flying transport aircraft, who would have been privileged women trained before the war,

Huge social changes take time to be accepted by everyone. Class distinctions could not be swept away overnight and they could still exist, causing misunderstandings and resentment. Lower class women resented the patronising treatment they received from those of more 'breeding' who quite often were totally useless at practical tasks having never learnt how to cook or do anything useful to the war effort. These differences given time tended to blur.

Keen as the women were to find work it took time for such enormous changes in society to become accepted. Naturally at first, the men resented the women 'taking their jobs'. Those men remaining in Britain tended to be older or highly skilled and the thinking must have been 'why should these young women with only a few weeks' training take over our jobs?' They resented women doing the same work as them. While the men may have had a point, it needs to be mentioned that the women were never paid the same, even when doing the same job.

Gun Factory at the Royal Arsenal, Woolwich London, 1918

A number of scandals were attached to the work in Munitions Factories. The Factory Acts which had been passed throughout the late 1800s to protect workers were no longer in force and the unhealthy conditions women faced were not acknowledged. Munitions workers, more than 750,000, were women, were often called canaries due to their yellow colouring which resulted from them working with TNT. This damaged their health, often seriously, those injured ran at 150,000 a year and for 400 the results were fatal.

Munitions being dangerous materials, explosions were known to have occurred in a number of factories. In an explosion on 5th December 1916 at Room 42 of the National Filling Station, Barnbow, 170 women were maimed or injured and 35 killed. Amazingly many of the women workers in that factory were so highly committed to their war work that within hours volunteers had moved back to work in Room 42.

Eight tons of TNT killed 134 people working at an explosion at Chilwell, Nottinghamshire; most of them were women. By 1917, reports of factory explosions in the press had been censored so it is difficult to know the true cost in human life.

As a diversion from the horror of the factory work many women workers chose to keep fit by playing football. Most factories had teams. A famous match was played on Christmas Day by the Dick Kerr Ladies Team of Lancashire. There were more than 10,000 spectators and it raised £600 to go towards, 'comforts for wounded soldiers'.

MAVIS AS A LAND GIRL was not always welcomed in farming communities. The problem being that many farmers had their own groups, their own ways of working and were struggling to meet demand. The land girls could give them an extra burden since the farmers would have been required to provide board and lodging for these young women who were from towns and cities and knew very little of the countryside.

Although the work was hard, many young women enjoyed themselves. They formed darts leagues and football teams and excelled at many activities, often surprising their hosts. Tractor driving and tractor maintenance were jobs where they were especially capable since some of the older farmers were sceptical about the new machines, of course—that was when tractors were available. Later in the war land girls often had to cope without tractors or horses since these were mostly requisitioned for the war effort. In such cases the women set about ploughing the fields by hand in the old way.

CHAPTER 10

LADY SOLDIERS!

WOMEN IN THE ARMED FORCES

APART FROM THE NURSING SERVICES women had never officially been employed to undertake work supporting the military overseas in war torn areas. The need for women in uniform, recruited and working in the same areas as the men was not realised until very late in World War 1. As with the nursing services, there were plenty of women involved in war work but the formation of the women's forces only happened on the back of many self funding organisations that had existed for years.

The **Women's Emergency Corp W.E.C**. was one such organisation and it was popular with government as it was a non-Suffrage group which trained unemployed women in occupations that were needed. W.E.C. had a number of areas in which Mavis worked and she became very popular. By Christmas 1914 the 'cooking department' had distributed 28,378 meals and 1,065 plum puddings. The organisation was also popular since unlike a number of supportive groups it welcomed women from all walks of life and all classes. **W.E.C.** provided interpreters to meet trains and boats from the continent offering support and accommodation to the 'poor souls' as they landed. They also provided dispatch riders and drivers who were able to do the running repairs on cars.

Sometime later in 1915 to meet the shortage of cooks and clerks in the Army a similar organisation, the **Women's Legion, W.L.**, was formed by the **Marchioness of Londonderry** which appealed to a large number of women (40,000 immediately registered to work). Although they started as voluntary, non-militaristic groups, W.L. and W.E.C. eventually evolved into the official female branch of the British Army.

The first women's branch of the British Army was known as **Women's Army Auxiliary Corps, WAACs** which also incorporated the nurses in the **Queen Mary's Army Auxiliary Corps** (1917).

The **Women's Royal Naval Service WRNS** followed in the same year, doing similar jobs as the WAACs. It included women working in signals, postal work, supplies, accounts and technical jobs and had 5,500 members, 500 of them officers. Apparently there existed an idea that WRNs were more ladylike than the WAACs, who knows? It is true they were given lessons in etiquette and applying make up.

The **Women's Royal Air Force (WRAF)** was formed in 1918 and for a short while recruited drivers and mechanics. It was disbanded in 1920. (The WRAF was reformed in 1949 and finally disbanded in 1994 when women were assimilated into the RAF proper.)

CONCLUSION

MAVIS MAY HAVE BEEN AVENGING the death of a spouse, searching for a loved one, needing to escape an unsavoury relationship or restricted life in Britain. She may have married a soldier or became caught up in wartime activities or she may have realized a need to reduce the suffering of war ravaged men.

On the home front she showed herself able to undertake many jobs possibly more successfully than the men. For example she seemed to have had a real aptitude for driving and lovingly caring for tractors.

I see WWI as a turning point in enabling the public to accept that women can do almost any job. It also made it obvious that women should have the vote. Although women over 30 with property were given the vote in 1918 it took another ten years until 1928 for all women over 21 to have the opportunity to vote.

It also has to be noted that although women had successfully undertaken the men's jobs during World Wars I and II, after both conflicts there was a push by government to encourage women back into their pre-war roles in order to free up their jobs for the returning men.

As I have shown, Mavis has, throughout history, affected the course of many wars through positive action. By the end of World War One it seemed there was hardly an occupation that women of all classes could not undertake.

AS A PASSING THOUGHT TO end this book I would like to mention a possible way forward for using women productively at times of war. Carol Colin in her book **Women and Wars** (2003) highlights a difficulty when using the United Nations peacekeepers. These peacekeeping troops often went into war ravaged situations. Their function was to disarm combatants, oversee the return of displaced people and make arrangements for the restarting of fuel and food supplies. Unfortunately they also caused another set of problems.

Evidence shows that male 'peacekeepers' not only failed to protect women from local men's violence but the women also became victims of exploitation at the hands of the UN troops. The rise of rape, sexual assault and prostitution in the vicinity of UN troops is well documented in a 2003 UN Bulletin 'Sexual Relationships between UN staff and Beneficiaries of Assistance'.

In 2015 there were in the Central African Republic 69 reported incidents of sexual assault and rape at the hands of the peacekeeping soldiers, compared to 52 cases the previous year. United Nations soldiers came from both European and African countries. The report by Hilary Margolis of Human Rights Watch does not mention the gender of the UN soldiers but they would have been predominantly male. Neither did she mention an interesting outcome from a previous UN involvement using women.

After a period of civil unrest when UN troops took over the situation in Liberia in 2007 the Blue Helmets which are intended to reassure a population were worn by a force of 140 Indian policewomen. A similar force of Bangladeshi women was used in Haiti.

In both situations when the women patrolled neighbourhoods there appeared to be greater trust among the local population. More illegal weapons were retrieved. There was no subsequent increase reported in sexual assaults or prostitution and associated crime.

Maybe this could be considered as a way forward for the future. Perhaps there is a greater role for female police forces in reducing aggression and the harmful effects of an influx of male troops.

MAVIS STILL EXISTS. I GUESS few young girls these days will be searching for a lost love, mobile phones and the internet give us an easier means of communication. But some of the reasons for joining the military will be similar to those of their forebears.

I am aware from my discussions with service men and women during the time of the First Gulf War that women, like many of the men, may not have seriously considered the possibility or consequences of killing another human being. Such is definitely not the motivation for many people be they male or female.

Young recruits tend to want adventure: to fly a plane, travel, learn new skills or to care for the wounded. We have female soldiers, sailors and airmen, diplomats and spies. Nowadays women can enter most professions. As far as employment opportunities are concerned there are more than there have ever been though maybe not yet enough. If they wish, women can become fighter pilots, can serve aboard submarines and service the most complex and sophisticated aircraft.

They can also indirectly join the military machine in the way women always have by marrying a serviceman. It is good to see The Military Wives Choir achieving a high profile in the media. This has given recognition to the unusual life the military wives also lead.

We, as women, have always been part of the war machinery. Thank goodness we are no longer invisible. I hope future war movies packed with daring action and heroism will include women and perhaps also those wives who 'Follow the Drum'. Maybe such films have already been made but I do not recall seeing too many.

REFERENCES

INTRODUCTION
Parker Chronicles (Anglo Saxon Chronicles)
Stansbury Don; (1993) *The Lady Who Fought the Vikings.*
Cardinal H.E.; (1983) *Orders of Knighthood and the Holy See.*

CHAPTER 1
Hilary Hind; (2011) *Early Quaker Culture.*
Holmes, Richard; editor (2001). *The Oxford Companion to Military History.*
Wheelwright Julie; (1990). *Amazons and Military Maids* (also chapter 2).
Florence Nightingale; National Portrait Gallery.
Mary Seacole; National Portrait Gallery.
Rudyard Kipling; (1896); *Soldiers' Stories—The Drums of Fore and Aft.*

CHAPTER 2
Military History Magazine: 1st October (2010).
The Army Children's Archives; TACA@www.archhistory.co.uk
Colonel NT St John Williams BA; (1971); *Tommy Atkins' Children—The Story of the Education of the Army's Children 1675-1970.*

CHAPTER 3
Myrna Trustram; (2008); *Women of the Regiment.*

CHAPTER 4

Barnes Alison; *The History of SSAFA*, Part 1: The Early Years.

CHAPTER 5

Dr. Vivien Newman; (2014): *We Also Served* (also Chapters 6& 7).

Diana Souhami; (2011); *Edith Cavell.*

The Telegraph / First World War Centenary—*Gabrielle Petit*; 4th July 2014.

Ruth Styles for *Mail Online*; 'The Incredible Story of Flora Sandes': 25th February 2014.

Sarah Oliver for *Mail Online*; 'Dorothy Lawrence; "She fought on the Somme disguised as a Tommy"'; 11th January 2014

CHAPTER 8&9

Neil R. Storey & Molly Housego; (2010); *Women in the First World War*; Shire Publications

ANNETTE BAILEY

BORN IN WW2, HER FATHER was a Catalina pilot and they did not know each other until she was 3 years old, his squadron being stationed in India. She is married to the novelist Garry Kilworth who was an R.A.F. cryptographer and they travelled as a military family living in Germany and the Mediterranean, often apart, sometimes for up to a year when he was abroad on active service.

In the early 1990s she was given the honorary rank of captain when she worked for the Royal Army Education Corp for 3 years. Her work was with military families in Hong Kong which she enjoyed enormously.

She has been a teacher, social worker, family therapist and tour guide. Her Master's degree concerned the experiences of children in military families. She still enjoys travelling with Garry and says she is fortunate to have two fine children and five terrific grandchildren.

Printed in Great Britain
by Amazon